Gooseberry Patch co.®

Y0-DKO-040

the Country Friends Collection®

Wrap · It · Up!

Holly... loves the challenge of wrapping an odd-shaped gift!

Mary Elizabeth... likes to tie a personal item to every gift box.

SPOTTY

GOURMET CANDY

Kate... prefers UN-wrapping to wrapping.

HELP.

Fear of Gift Wrapping

Wrap·o·pHOBIA— an extreme terror related to gift wrapping, brought on by lack of organization and missing tape and scissors.

2

In a perfect world, your giftwrap supplies would all be neatly organized in a lovely antique walnut armoire. The kids would never use your $12.per.yard, wired, organza ribbon as a leash for the dog... your husband wouldn't dream of borrowing your scissors to pry the lid off a can of paint... the tape would never run out, tissue wouldn't get wrinkly, raffia wouldn't be tied in a zillion knots.

But this is the REAL WORLD.

The best we can do is try, try, try to keep the BASICS on hand and in some semblance of ORDER.

Here's HOW:

1. Find a big old container.

A BIG HONKER OF A TRASH CAN WORKS GREAT...

... OR A GIANT CLEAR PLASTIC STORAGE BOX.

This is to hold all your rolls of giftwrap neatly.

2. Now find a good, sturdy basket or box.

Keep all your ribbons and trims in it. (If you pick a pretty container, maybe you'll be more likely to keep it more organized....nah. Better get a no-see-throug box with a lid.)

3. Put your hands on a big bucket.

It's the handiest thing to hold scissors, pens, rulers, and tools. Use a heavy iron chain to attach your scissors to the bucket handle so nobody "borrows" them.

4. Hide it all.

Maybe in a dark corner of the cellar. Or the laundry room. Somewhere nobody but YOU ever goes.

KEEP OUT

5. Locate a clear, flat surface on which to work.

This may be difficult in a busy household. Hire a bulldozer to clean off the dining room table, or simply use a card table if that works better.

Ok...

you're almost

ready...

the ESSENTIALS

ROLLS OF WRAPPING PAPER

TISSUE PAPER

GIFT BAGS in a VARIETY of SIZES

ROLLS OF TAPE

A HOLE PUNCHER

RIBBON, RIBBON, RIBBON!

A handful of ready-made BOWS

WIRE CUTTERS

TAGS

PENS and MARKERS

...and MANY pairs of scissors!

More Good Stuff for your giftwrap Hide·Away:

* GLUE GUN and GLUE STICKS
* YARN, JUTE, STRING, WIRES
* OLD BEADS, JEWELRY PIECES, SILK FLOWERS, LEAVES, METAL CHARMS and VINTAGE JUNK FOR PACKAGE TOPPERS
* FABRIC, NETTING, SEWING NOTIONS
* RUBBER STAMPING EQUIPMENT
* GLITTER, SEQUINS & SPARKLY GARLANDS and GEMS TO GLUE ON
* A RADIO OR CD PLAYER FOR LOVELY BACKGROUND MUSIC!
* FOLDING RACK TO HOLD TISSUE OR GIFTWRAP
* INTERESTING PAPERS ～ FOILS & TEXTURED SHEETS FROM A SCRAPBOOK STORE ARE FUN FOR WRAPPING OR TAGGING!
* FANCY·EDGED SCISSORS
* TOOL BOX TO HOLD TEENY PIECES OF TRIMS & BEADS

7

IT'S NOT THAT HARD! KATE MAKES A FANCY BOW IN

BOW KNOW-HOW

Learn to tie bows
   the Country Friends' way
and soon you'll be *looping*
            and *curling* all day...

   Practice makes perfect
      so give it a whirl
         Soon you'll have lovely
            loops, knots and curls!

Start with a
roll of wired
ribbon. Unroll
it so it's easy
to work with.
Fold the ribbon
back and forth
and make a "stack" of
three loops, each one
about 6" or 7" long. Leave the
ribbon "tails" as long as the loops.

1

2.

"Pinch" the loops smack in the middle with a pipe cleaner — just tie it to keep the loops from escaping!

3.

Now tie a couple of 12" to 15" pieces of curling ribbon right over the pipe cleaner knot. Curl the ends with scissors 'til you have cute *Curly·cues!* Trim and shape your bow as needed — no obsessing, now.

4.

Here's the fun part: hot·glue a neat charm, teeny ornament, even a dog treat, right in the center of the bow! Fiddle with the loops a little, just so everything looks just right, then plop it on a gift and go!

It does not matter how slowly you go, so long as you do not stop. — CONFUCIUS

What a lovely box

She will notice that you took the extra time and effort to wrap your gift *beautifully*.

⚘ Save silk flower blossoms and greens to hot glue on a box instead of a bow... shiny white paper with a white satin ribbon and a big white silk cabbage rose makes a package *almost* too pretty to open.

⚘ Buy a floral tube at your neighborhood flower shop... it's a small plastic vial that holds water and a single bloom. Wire it to a box or handle of a gift bag, insert one lovely daisy and you're good to go and give.

Top a glossy wrap with a doily ～ paper or lace ～ then add a beautiful bow. Try pale pink paper and bow with a vintage ecru doily for a very *feminine* touch.

Slide *Beads* on a shiny gold wire for a pretty "ribbon".

Use a tube of gold glitter glue (available at craft shops) to decorate a simple papier maché hatbox. Paint the box a rich ruby red; let dry. Make scrolls and squiggles of gold with the glitter glue on the box. Finish it off with an extravagant bow of wired ribbon and a sprig of gold foil leaves from a cake decorating store. *Oh! So flamboyant!*

Sew up a simple "envelope" of organza, chiffon or another semi-sheer fabric. Slide a small gift inside ～ jewelry, a poem, a journal or book ～ and fasten shut with a pretty little pin or a ribbon tied 'round.

11

Straps and Scraps and

Sew some gingham ribbons to a plain old paper lunch bag for swingy straps!

Glue on a fabric initial from plaid or calico scraps ~ an easy country monogram.

Save your coffee cans! You can drop a sealed bag of homemade cookies inside the can and gather a big square of burlap 'round it. Use a heavy rubber band to catch the burlap at the top, then tie a generous loop of raffia or a thin strip of bandanna fabric over the rubber band. Hot glue a jaunty silk sunflower over the knot for a down-home homemade gift!

Use leftover wallpaper to cut out giant initials ~ wet·and· stick on a wrapped giftbox for a clever topper.

Flaps and Maps and Burlaps

Pop a gift inside a colored paper bag. Fold top over to make a flap. Make a pair of holes with your paper punch through the flap and the bag (you can use metal eyelets, available in scrapbook supply shops, if you are especially crafty), then thread three or four different yarns or neat textured threads through the holes. Tie the fibers into a knot to keep the bag shut, and add a cool charm to the longest piece of thread.

Wrap with a MAP! For a great going-away gift, select a map of where she's going... top off the box with a pair of kids' binoculars, an inexpensive compass or a tiny toy car.

Wrap a gift for a milestone birthday in "memory" paper: make copies of her high school yearbook pages for giftwrap! She'll have a giggle over the silly photos.

the Presentation is half of the fun!

KATE

★ KEEP YOUR eyes OPEN AT TAG SALES FOR INTERESTING OLD PURSES and BILLFOLDS ∿ YOU CAN LOAD UP A GRANDMA-STYLE BAG WITH ALL KINDS OF GOODIES (vintage hankie, mints, all the junk your granny hauled around). OLD BAGS and WALLETS CAN BE REVIVED WITH FABRIC PAINTS, DECOUPAGED PICTURES and GLUED-ON BEADS JUST FOR FUN.

★ THERE ARE <u>SO</u> MANY NEAT PAPER NAPKINS AVAILABLE! TRIM A FUN ONE TO FIT AROUND A CLEAR JAR OF HOMEMADE JELLY; OVERLAP THE EDGES JUST SLIGHTLY AND GLUE IT ON, USING A RUBBER BAND TO KEEP IT ON WHILE IT DRIES. (Be careful or rubber band will tear the napkin) SMALL FLAGS WORK GREAT, TOO!

★ WRAP A BOTTLE WITH A TEXTURED PAPER FROM YOUR STACK OF SCRAPBOOK SHEETS ∿ MAKE A SLEEVE OF CORRUGATED CARDBOARD OR AN EMBOSSED CARD STOCK, and KEEP IT CLOSED WITH DOUBLE-STICK TAPE and A WRAP OF SILK CORD. SLIDE SOME VERY INTERESTING BEADS ON THE CORD ENDS, THEN KNOT THEM TIGHT.

Why, That is un·heard of!

(and I LIKE it!)

Use your noggin to think of new ways to use everyday stuff for fun wraps:

SKIP THE HO·HUM GIFT BASKET.

Fill a SHOWER CAP

WITH A BUNCH OF BATH·TIME BEAUTY TOYS—

BOTTLES OF BATH GEL • RUBBER DUCK • LOTIONS & SOAKS • WASH CLOTH • A GREAT RAZOR

SEW AN EXTRAVAGANT RIBBON and RUFFLE OF WIDE EYELET OR LACE TO A PAIR OF

RUBBER GLOVES.

GLUE ON A HUMONGOUS "DIAMOND" and STUFF THE GLOVES WITH HAND LOTION TUBES and KITCHEN UTENSILS ↝ a FUN SHOWER GIFT.

POKE A STACK OF LINENS OR FAIRY TALE BOOKS INSIDE A

Pillowcase

YOU'VE PERSONALIZED WITH RUBBER STAMPS and FABRIC PAINTS. (THAT'S A FUN WAY TO GIVE A PAIR OF JAMMIES AS WELL!)

☆ Sweet ☆ Dreams Molly!

An idea is SALVATION by IMAGINATION. – FRANK LLOYD WRIGHT

BeHOLD the PLASTIC BAG.

→EVERY GIFT-WRAPPER'S BEST FRIEND←

IT'S QUICK.
IT'S THRIFTY.
IT'S EASY.

★ WRAP THE GIFT IN COLORED TISSUE PAPER. DROP IN BAG and TIE WITH A TRIO OF BRIGHT RIBBONS. GREAT FOR HARD-TO-WRAP STUFF!

★ FILL SMALL CLEAR BAGS WITH COLORFUL CANDIES and TWIST A PIPE CLEANER 'ROUND THE TOPS TO KEEP THE YUMMIES INSIDE! (THIS WORKS FOR PLATES OF COOKIES, TOO)

★ A GREAT KITCHEN SHOWER GIFT: BUY A PLASTIC DISH DRAINER. PILE IT FULL OF KITCHEN JUNK ∽ SPATULAS, SCRUBBIES, PLASTIC STORAGE BOWLS, SQUIRTY MUSTARD-AND-KETCHUP BOTTLES ∽ANYTHING COLORFUL IS GOOD. SLIDE THE WHOLE THING INSIDE A BIG PLASTIC BAG and TIE IT SHUT WITH A RIBBON OF TULLE and A-DISH-SCRUBBER-ON-A-STICK.

happy shower!

★ GLUE A FUNNY PHOTO OF YOURSELF TO A PLASTIC BAG. USE A BOLD MAGIC MARKER TO WRITE A "TO and FROM" MESSAGE ON THE PHOTO, and SLIDE A TISSUE-WRAPPED GIFT INSIDE. FOLD BAG OVER and CLOSE WITH WIDE CLEAR TAPE.

Love, Kate

3 Clever Ways to Disguise a Gift Certificate

1. HIDE A GIFT CARD TO A LOCAL MUSIC SHOP INSIDE AN OLD RECORD ALBUM COVER. HAVE FUN AT A THRIFT SHOP LOOKING FOR A CORNY COVER!

BACH'S Greatest ★HITS★ for AccordiaN

TAPE THE GIFT CARD TO THE RECORD. JUST ADD A RIBBON!

2.  SLIDE A GIFT CERTIFICATE FOR A FAVORITE BOOKSTORE INSIDE AN ANTIQUE BOOK. (THEY ARE READILY AVAILABLE AND VERY INEXPENSIVE AT SECOND-HAND SHOPS & FLEA MARKETS.) FIND A TITLE THAT FITS WHO YOU'RE GIVING IT TO; A GARDEN BOOK FOR A FLOWER BUFF, OR A VINTAGE ROMANCE NOVEL FOR A FICTION READER. TIE IT UP WITH A NEAT BOOKMARK ON A RIBBON.

OH DEAR!

3. FIND THE MOST HIDEOUS PIECE OF CLOTHING EVER MANUFACTURED ON YOUR NEXT GARAGE SALE TREASURE HUNT. TUCK A GIFT CERTIFICATE TO A HIP CLOTHING STORE INSIDE THE POCKET OF THOSE GREEN & YELLOW PLAID POLYESTER PANTS! WRAP THE WHOLE THING IN CLASHING PAPER & RIBBON.

Something DiFFeRENt

...when regular just won't do.

instead of PAPER, Try:

- antique hankies
- color copies of kids' artwork or handwritten letters
- newspapers
- comic pages
- foil

riBBoN replacements:

- seam binding
- rick·rack
- colorful electric wire
- rope ★ thin chain
- a boa
- Christmas tree garland
- rubber bands

terrific toppers:

- little toys
- beauty goods- hand mirror, small brush, hair barrettes
- buttons
- fishing lures & bobbers
- golf tees
- office supplies

bright polka dot wrap, neon pink boa and a sweet little hand mirror on top

glossy green paper, fishing line "ribbon" and 2 red plastic bobbers!

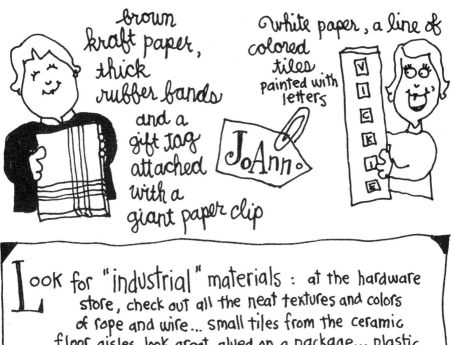

brown kraft paper, thick rubber bands and a gift tag attached with a giant paper clip

JoAnn

white paper, a line of colored tiles painted with letters

VICKIE

Look for "industrial" materials : at the hardware store, check out all the neat textures and colors of rope and wire... small tiles from the ceramic floor aisles look great glued on a package... plastic clothespins or old wooden ones are cool "clippies" to attach a tag... bolts, nuts and washers can be glued on top of a gift, used on tags or tied on the ends of ribbons.

Wander around the office supply store with an open mind!

There's a goldmine of materials in them-thar aisles:
* paperclips (make a chain!) * tags & price stickers & labels
* rubber stamps (have one made to order) * tablet papers

Keep your eyes open ∽ giftwrap possibilities are where you least expect them!

So, you see, imagination needs moodling ∽ long, inefficient, happy idling, dawdling and puttering. - BRENDA UELAND-

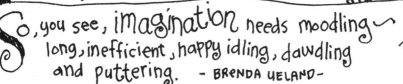

19

sit down and make a stack of TAGS.

Here are a bunch of Country Friends tags. →
Make copies of 'em, as many as you want.

Then wHat?

First things first. Make a batch o'

Cashew Crunch

to keep the creative
juices flowing.

a recipe from Dianne Gregory
★ Sheridan, AR ★

½ c. butter
1 c. sugar
1·½ c. cashews

Combine all ingredients in a
saucepan. Heat over high heat,
stirring constantly until
color has turned to a
light tan. Pour into
buttered jelly-roll pan; set
aside to cool. Break into
bite·size pieces. Makes 1·½ cups.

thanks

love

friend

20

Just for YOU.

Love you Bunches.

Just Because.

glad you're my
friend.

tHanks
for making me giggle.

I think you're
neAT.

OK, now that you've got a stack of copies,

make them yours.

(You don't want them to look just
like everybody else's, do you?)

Suggestions:

* use decorative-edged scissors and trim the tags ∽ layer them on a different color/texture/patterned paper.

* Use a glittery paint to sparkle up your cards.

Just for you.

* Glue on a tiny charm or add stickers.

make a Christmas ☆ Wish.

* Use embroidery floss to sew a simple running·stitch border around the card.

girl friend.

* Sew a little chiffon "envelope" and slip the tag inside. Before you sew it shut, add a small pinch of glitter, sequins or confetti.
(write a little note on the back of the tag, too!)

Love.

☆ 22

* Layer a little piece of vellum paper over the tag for a dreamy look, then glue on teeny·tiny beads.

have the very

merriest!

Happy day!

I
really, really, really
Like you.

Joy
to
the
world.

make a
Christmas
WiSH.

girl
friend

Homemade Hand Lotion

...a potion from Michelle Campen
★ Peoria, IL ★

¼ c. rosewater
¼ c. glycerin
2 T. witch hazel
1 T. almond oil

Combine ingredients together; mix well. Pour into a small bottle or jar. Makes about ½ cup.

Little hands will love measuring, mixing and pouring ... with adult supervision, of course.

KID CRAFTS:

"Look what I made!"

Gather a group of your favorite little girlfriends. make and wrap a bottle of homemade lotion for each gal to take home for mom!

Life is a great bundle of little things.
—OLIVER WENDELL HOLMES—

homemade Hand Lotion

Make copies of these labels to glue or tape to your bottles after you fill them with lotion. You may want to adjust the size of the labels ⌣ and certainly you'll want to color them up!

Gather a square of tulle up 'round your lotion bottle and tie a satin bow!

Pink Lemonade
FOR THIRSTY GIRLIES

WHIRL REGULAR SUGAR IN A BLENDER TO MAKE IT SUPERFINE.

22 Lemons, Halved & Squeezed
2 c. Superfine sugar
4 c. cold water
4 c. crushed ice
½ c. cranberry juice

♥

Pour lemon juice in a large pitcher; stir in sugar until dissolved. Add water & cranberry juice; stir in crushed ice. Serve immediately. Makes 10 servings.

25

Candy Rolls

...a good idea from
Susan McClusker ✶ Las Vegas

✶

YOU'LL NEED:

PAPER TOWEL ROLL, CUT IN HALF
10·½" × 7" PIECE OF FABRIC
TAPE OR GLUE
2 12" LENGTHS OF RIBBON
ASSORTED SMALL CANDIES

✶

Center roll on fabric edge;
roll up and adhere in place with
tape or glue. Twist fabric on one
end and tie closed with ribbon.
Fill roll with candy; twist and
close fabric with remaining
ribbon. Makes one.

♡ I ♡
like you
even more than
candy.
♡

Here's a
tag to copy,
color and
tie on your
candy roll.

Example has more
followers than
reason.
- CHRISTIAN BOVEE -

Collage!

ABCDEFGHIJK
LMNOPQRST
UVWXYZ ★ ♥
1234567890

and to from love

Copy this alphabet and fun drawings... let the kids cut out the letters and collage them on plain old cartons, boxes, tubes, jars and bags... ransom~note style!

idea:

forget that old saying... good things sometimes come in **BIG** packages.

Find an enormous box. Fill it with styrofoam peanuts. Giftwrap a tiny present in a tiny box and hide it in the peanuts. Now seal the gigantic box.

Kids especially will enjoy diving into all those messy peanuts for a tiny treasure hunt.

★ (Pat yourself on the back for being creative, fun-loving and for recycling.)

I tried thinking outside the box but I just ended up in a bigger BOX.

—Lisa Smith—

red roller

the "How will I ever disguise that??" dilemma:

The answer is: **Don't.**

Use wrap, duct tape, whatever it takes to make a form-fitting cover for that hard-to-disguise present, like tricycles, golf clubs, bowling balls! (good for a giggle)

Homemade Wrappin'
is extra special.

A big sheet of white butcher paper or brown kraft paper can be jazzed up on-the-cheap for unique wrappings:

Fingerpaint a design.

Stencil or **R**ubber-stamp a pattern on paper.

Cartoon on it ~ everyone's an artist.

Hand-write a message all over the paper!

Merry Ch
Kate! I hope
you like this
special for you
Have ★

Recycle!

We're not suggesting you go **DUMPSTER DIVING** ... (unless you just <u>WANT</u> to).

Simply take a closer look at the stuff you're throwing away! There's plenty of clever **re·usable RUBBISH** in there that makes mighty fine wrappings:

merry

HI

JOY

★ Empty egg cartons are fun to spray paint and fill with treasures: try a six-pack of socks, a dozen golf balls or a handfull of gourmet candies in the "holes".

★ Newspapers and magazines offer a wealth of clip-out-and-tape-on **letters.**

★ Turn a foil tater chip bag inside out~ wash it up and stash full of goodies!

★ Wash the labels off jars and glue on your own. Decorate with fun **Stickers.**

YUM

HOLLY'S
Paper Dollies

So simple! So cute glued on
a kraft-paper-wrapping!

Ok, find an old newspaper ↝ the want ads will do
nicely. If it's not already old and yellowed, tea-dye it
and lay it flat to dry. (some wrinkles and waves are fine ↝ we're
striving for an "old paper" look). Now, lay down a copy of the
patterns above and cut the snowman or gingerbread boy out of
the new-old newspaper. Glue on plain black buttons for eyes
and trim, then glue your boys on a box you've wrapped in simple
brown kraft paper. Tie on a plain black grosgrain ribbon to finish.

InDeX

Has anybody seen my Scissors?

When you rise in the morning, form a resolution to make the day a happy one for a fellow creature. ~ SYDNEY SMITH

GIFT-WRAP A LITTLE SURPRISE TO LEAVE ON SOMEONE's BREAKFAST PLATE!